16.90

THE SEARCH FOR THE KILLER ASTEROID

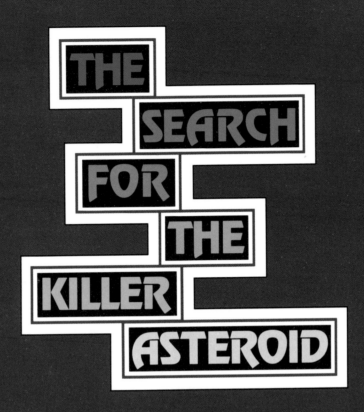

GREGORY L. VOGT

THE MILLBROOK PRESS
BROOKFIELD, CONNECTICUT

With considerable respect and admiration
for her leadership, talents, and passion
for education, I dedicate this book to
Pamela M. Bacon, my friend and colleague.

THE SEARCH FOR THE KILLER ASTEROID

CRETACEOUS MORNING!

Swirls of morning mist drifted gently across the swampy southern end of the long lake. The sky over the distant eastern ridge changed from black to red and then to yellow as the first of the sun's rays streaked across the land. Small flowering plants opened their blooms, and ferns slowly bent their fronds eastward to capture the sunlight. As a breeze picked up, the nearby forest of pine, cycad, and palm trees began to sway. Off in the distance *Pteranodons* flapped their giant leathery wings to gain altitude and catch rising warm air currents. Farther still, a shadowy pair of *Triceratops* began their breakfast of fern leaves. Except for the noise of the wind, all was silent until the snorting began. The old leader of the *Parasaurolophus* herd was the first to stir, and he roused the others with his deep foghornlike calls. It was time for breakfast.

Old Paras stretched more than 33 feet (10 meters) from the tip of his bill-like mouth to the end of his long, flattened tail. He started moving warily on four legs toward the forest. His hind legs were large and powerful, and when he had to escape a predator, he could run upright with his small front legs held in the air. In the running position, his long neck and long tail balanced his massive body, making him look like a bumpy seesaw.

Because of the shape of their mouths, we call the dinosaur family to which Old Paras and the rest of his herd belonged the *hadrosaur*, or duck-billed, family. It was a widespread family with many different members, told apart by the shape of their skulls. The male *Parasaurolophus* had a narrow crest of bone extending from the front of the skull for more than 3 feet (1 meter) behind the back. The crest gently hooked downward to make the skull resemble the head of a tack hammer. Female crests were shorter and more sharply curved. Inside the mouths of duckbills were many closely packed teeth. The teeth were rough like a carpenter's wood rasp—perfect for grinding and pulverizing tough pine needles and branches to make them easier to digest.

As he moved closer to the forest, Old Paras scanned the trees, looking for predators. If a *Tyrannosaurus rex* or an *Albertosaurus* was hiding there, the herd would have to retreat to the protection of the deep lake. Their thick feet and broad tails would propel them through the water to safety. Fleeing was their only defense.

The herd following the leader to the forest edge consisted of ten adults and one juvenile. In a good year, there would be three or four youngsters, but an attack by a pack of *Albertosauruses* the week before had left the herd with only one juvenile female.

Young Paras began scampering around the front of the herd. Bouncing and running, she earned a few angry snorts from the leader. Old Paras wasn't in the mood for *Parasaurolophus* play.

As the herd settled into eating, Young Paras darted from tree to tree, biting off lower pine needles while the adults reached up to the taller branches. Young Paras occasionally got ahead of the herd to get the first bites off new trees. A snort from the leader reminded her to come back, but then Old Paras got too involved in his own breakfast to notice that she was getting farther and farther away.

Back several yards from the edge of the forest stood an old *T. rex*. He was over 40 feet (12 meters) long, stood 18 feet (5.5 meters) tall, and weighed more than seven tons. *T. rex* stood very still. His greenish brown, pebbly hide helped him blend in with the surrounding trees—his stout legs looked like fat tree trunks. Only his large eyes and forehead were visible through a gap in the branches.

T. rex's massive, bony head was 3 feet (1 meter) long. When he made a kill, he would plow into his prey at a speed of more than 20 miles (32 kilometers) per hour. The impact of the head alone was usually enough to break the victim's bones and disable it, but *T. rex* had another weapon. His mouth was lined with rows of curved dagger-size teeth that were perfect for ripping away hundred-pound chunks of flesh and bones.

T. rex remained motionless, taking quick, shallow breaths to be as quiet as possible. Although he preferred an adult duckbill, the young *Parasaurolophus* was coming his way. In *T. rex*'s younger days, he would have broken cover by this time and run down the juvenile. Back then, he had hunted in packs with other young *T. rexes*. One *T. rex* would start the chase, and others would take over in turn until the victim was exhausted. Then, the kill. Old *T. rex* could still outrun most duckbills, but his adult bulk limited his range. It was surer to wait just a little bit longer. Young Paras continued to move closer and finally came up to a fresh tree just a few *T. rex* steps away from the hiding place.

T. rex let out a deep throaty bellow and lunged forward. For a moment, Young Paras froze in her steps. But when the pine trees in front of her splintered as *T. rex* began plowing through them, Young Paras turned and started running. The older and more experienced

A *Tyrannosaurus rex* threatens a pair of smaller dinosaurs.

members of the *Parasaurolophus* herd didn't bother to look in Young Paras's direction. *T. rex*'s roars and thunderous steps and Young Paras's high-pitched cries told them all they needed to know. Everyone started running for the water. There was nothing else they could do.

T. rex opened his jaws and aimed for Young Paras's neck. With every long tyrannosaur stride, he shortened the distance—just a few more steps. But suddenly, a dark shadow appeared overhead. *T. rex* hesitated. Perhaps from deep in his memory came a vision of younger days, when a bigger *T. rex* would drive him away from a kill he had just made. Without thinking, he turned his head to look at his challenger. But instead of a bigger *T. rex*, he could see only a huge, dark, boiling cloud rapidly covering the sun. *T. rex* turned to continue the chase but, in his moment of hesitation, Young Paras had gained several steps and was already entering the water. It was too late to catch her.

T. rex broke into a trot and paced along the edge of the water. He roared and snorted angrily at the herd and then walked back into the forest. There was always tomorrow.

The dark cloud grew larger and blotted out more of the sky. Then the land began to shake. *T. rex* and the other dinosaurs were knocked to the ground as a huge, thunderous earthquake buckled the land, opening chasms, toppling tall trees, and spilling water out of the long lake. More tremors followed in wave after wave.

An hour later, the boom came. It sounded like thunder, but it echoed across the land for many minutes. The boom was followed by unbearably hot winds. The splintered forests on the ridge tops caught fire and burned throughout the night.

The next morning daylight never came. There was just a hint of gray in the sky where the sun should have been; the rest of the sky was dark. The cloud now stretched from horizon to horizon. Hot, dry winds whipped the forest around the lake and drove large waves across to the far shore. Lightning ignited more fires, bringing light back to the dismal landscape. Acrid smoke filled the air. It was the same the next day and the next. Then, heavy rains began. The acid content of the rain was so high that trees and ferns that had been missed by the fires suffered.

Without the sun's energy, the land grew cold. Rain turned to snow. The few remaining green plants on the land could no longer make food, and they began to die. For a time, the *Parasaurolophus* herd lived off the energy contained in their bodies, but without food they began to die too. Young Paras was the first to go, and then the older *Parasaurolophus* followed. Old *T. rex* and other meat eaters survived longer by scavenging the carcasses of the plant eaters. Finally, there were no more carcasses to eat, and the last of the meat eaters died as well.

Life in the oceans didn't fare any better. Acid rain washed out to sea, poisoning the waters. Floating plants died, and the animals that ate the plants died along with them. So did the animals that ate the animals.

Many months later, the clouds thinned and the sun gradually reappeared. Its light fell upon a new world. Dinosaurs, which had held dominion over the land for 160 million years, were gone. And gone, too, were more than 70 percent of all the living species on Earth. No animals bigger than small dogs survived.

SIXTY-FIVE MILLION YEARS LATER

The job of a geologist is to try to discover how Earth formed; how its mountains, valleys, basins, plains, oceans, continents, and islands came to be. It's a challenging job because it takes geologists backward in time. They start with the way Earth is today and try to reconstruct the events that led up to the present. It is an approach that is something like looking at a completed jigsaw puzzle and trying to decide which piece was laid down first, which one second, and so on. There are some rules that help geologists with their puzzle. For example, if there are two layers of rock formed from sediments that piled up on the floor of an ocean long ago, the rock layer on top is usually the younger.

In the summer of 1973, Walter Alvarez and some other geologists were in central Italy, studying thick layers of ancient pinkish limestone. The rock began accumulating in the ocean 155 million years ago in the Jurassic period, when dinosaurs roamed our planet. Sedimentation continued through the Cretaceous period and into the Tertiary period, ending 30 million years ago in the Oligocene epoch. By then, all the dinosaurs had become extinct.

A thin, pale band of clay marks the K-T boundary, between the Cretaceous and Tertiary periods.

The Italian limestone was like a giant time machine. By starting at its topmost layer and working downward, Alvarez and his colleagues could travel backward through 125 million years of Earth's history. Part way down from the top, at the 65-million-year level, was an insignificant-looking layer of reddish gray clay less than 1 inch (2.5 centimeters) thick. The layer was hardly insignificant. It was what geologists have named the K-T boundary—the boundary between the Cretaceous and Tertiary periods.

A MYSTERIOUS LINE ▪ The K-T boundary exists not only in Italy but in many places around the world. Beneath it are found dinosaur fossils and fossils of many other extinct forms of plant and marine life. But above that layer, no dinosaur fossils are present. Neither are found most of the other life forms that flourished during the age of reptiles. It was as though a great eraser wiped most living things off the surface of Earth, so that life had to start over again. That thin K-T boundary marked the point in time when those extinctions took place.

Alvarez and his colleagues had originally come to Italy to learn about the Earth's ancient magnetic field. By studying magnetic elements within the Italian limestone, they could learn the directions and strength of the magnetic field through history. But as Alvarez came across the K-T boundary, he became fascinated. Since the thin clay layer marked the time when a great period of extinctions took place, Alvarez began to wonder what it could tell about how the dinosaurs and the other Cretaceous animals and plants had died.

Back in the United States, Alvarez involved his father in his new questions. Luis Alvarez, a scientist who specialized in the study of cosmic rays and atomic particles, caught his son's enthusiasm and became intrigued with the K-T boundary also. One of the first questions the father and son team asked was how many years the thin clay layer had taken to form. The layer's thinness meant that it had probably formed quickly, unlike the limestone below and above it.

To answer their question, they decided to do a little detective work and look for dust. You can get an idea of how long ago a house was last cleaned by looking at the dust on tabletops. If there isn't any dust, the house was just cleaned. But if there are thick layers of dust, the last cleaning was months or even years ago. The Alvarezes didn't look for household dust; they examined the K-T clay layer for iridium dust. The element iridium is relatively rare in the rocks of Earth's

Luis and Walter Alvarez examine a rock sample showing the K-T layer.

crust, but it is quite common in meteoroids in space. Every day, meteor dust, containing iridium, falls to Earth at a more or less constant rate. This dust is incorporated into sedimentary rocks as they form. By checking how much iridium was contained in the clay layer, they would have a crude clock that would help them estimate how long it took for the clay layer to form.

As they ran their chemical tests, the Alvarez team was astonished to discover that the clay layer contained thirty times the iridium it should have held. Something interesting had taken place.

Walter Alvarez returned to Italy in 1978 to get more samples. He collected an entire sequence of rocks beginning below the K-T layer and ending above it. Tests on the rocks above and below the K-T layer showed a constant amount of iridium, but the K-T layer again showed a great concentration. The new tests confirmed that the concentration was thirty times greater in the K-T layer than in the rocks below or above it.

The next question the Alvarezes asked was whether this iridium concentration was unique to Italy or occurred elsewhere too. Samples of the K-T clay layer found in Denmark and even all the way around the world, in K-T rocks found in New Zealand, also contained the heavy iridium concentration. It seemed that the concentration of iridium in the K-T layer was worldwide.

A NEW THEORY ▪ Over the years, many scientists have tried to explain why the dinosaurs disappeared. Their explanations have ranged from the commonplace to the silly. Some have suggested that worldwide volcanic activity filled Earth's upper atmosphere with dust, blocking sunlight for many years and eventually killing plants and dinosaurs. Others have suggested that the dinosaurs just evolved into other life forms that are living today. In still another idea, dinosaurs were on the decline, for various reasons, and just naturally died out. Small mammals may have led to the dinosaurs' extinction because of their voracious appetites for dinosaur eggs. One of the strangest hypotheses suggested that certain plants that dinosaurs ate helped them with digestion. When the plants became extinct, the dinosaurs died of constipation! None of these hypotheses was very satisfactory because there was no way any of them could be scientifically tested.

The discovery of iridium in the K-T layer led the Alvarez team to their own hypothesis. They concluded the high concentration of iridium in the very thin K-T layer must have formed all at once. They hypothesized that a huge *asteroid*, or space rock, fell to Earth from space. At least 6 miles (10 kilometers) in diameter and bursting through the Earth's atmosphere at a speed of 60,000 miles (almost 100,000 kilometers) per hour, the asteroid would have blasted out a *crater* in Earth's surface more than 100 miles (about 160 kilometers) wide! The asteroid and the rock it struck would have been pulverized into fine dust and thrown into Earth's upper atmosphere. Quickly spreading out, the dust would have turned day into night for the entire planet. *Photosynthesis*, the sunlight-driven process by which plants take in water and carbon dioxide and make food and oxygen, would cease. Plants would die, and the animals that depend on them would follow. In time, the dust, rich in iridium, would have settled, blanketing Earth's surface. The dust would have become a thin clay layer all over Earth's surface.

The Alvarez hypothesis made sense to many scientists, although not all scientists agreed with it. At least, everyone thought, this hypothesis provided something to start with, something that could be investigated. If investigations confirmed the asteroid impact, a great question that has intrigued scientists for many years would be solved. Even if their investigations proved that the Alvarez hypothesis was not correct, researchers might still discover other clues that could lead them to the real reasons for the extinction.

Scientists began searching for proofs for the Alvarez hypothesis, especially what some people called the "smoking gun." In a shooting case, a person holding a smoking gun is usually assumed to be the one who fired it even if no one saw the shot being fired. If a giant asteroid did strike Earth and kill the dinosaurs, it should have left a telltale crater. Even with *erosion*, the wearing away of the Earth's surface by wind, water, and ice, there should still be faint markings

ASTEROIDS, COMETS, AND METEOROIDS

The solar system is more complicated than many people realize. While its main occupants are the sun, planets, and moons, the solar system—the region surrounding the sun for about one-third the distance to the nearest star—is host to trillions of other objects. These objects are *asteroids, comets*, and *meteoroids*.

Asteroids are pieces of space rock and metal ranging from a few tens of yards to about 600 miles (almost 1,000 kilometers) in diameter. Several thousand asteroids have been discovered; most orbit the sun in a broad region between Mars and Jupiter. Occasionally, some of these asteroids collide and shatter into millions of smaller pieces that are called meteoroids. Blasted into new orbits by the impact, some meteoroids may eventually reach Earth and burn up in its atmosphere or survive all the way to the surface. Then the meteoroids are called *meteors* or *meteorites.*

Collisions are not the only forces that send objects into new orbits. Jupiter's powerful gravitational pull, several times greater than Earth's, can throw asteroids that come too near into new orbits that bring them into the inner solar system. If they cross Earth's orbit, they are called *Earth-crossing asteroids*, or ECAs.

Comets are less solid than asteroids and contain ice. Many comets orbit in the outer fringes of the solar system. The orbits of some, however, are so elliptical, or egg-shaped, that they are carried near the sun and then back into space, usually beyond the orbit of Jupiter. As a comet approaches the sun, the sun's heat melts some of the ice, creating vapor that streams behind the comet to form a tail sometimes millions of miles long. Comets that cross Earth's orbit are called *Earth-crossing comets*, or ECCs. Together, ECAs and ECCs are called *near-Earth objects*, or NEOs.

somewhere created by the impact that triggered the mass extinctions. The crater couldn't be just any large hole. It had to have been created by an impact 65 million years ago and be at least 100 miles (about 160 kilometers) in diameter. However, no crater of the right age and size was known to the scientists who began looking for the "smoking gun." Where was the crater?

THE SMOKING GUN

The forces of erosion are powerful. Wind, running water, flowing glaciers, chemical action, gravity, temperature changes, and even plant and animal life wear away the rock that makes up our planet. Ancient mountain chains once as big as North America's Rocky Mountains have been worn down to low hills. Over several million years, the Colorado River has scoured away rock to create the Grand Canyon, a chain of interweaving canyons a mile (1.6 kilometers) deep in places. Further changing Earth's surface are the forces that slowly but constantly move the roughly fifteen large plates that make up the planet's outer layers. Where the plates collide, the land is uplifted to form new mountains and volcanoes that spread their lava and ash to cover the surface.

It was not too surprising to many scientists that it might be difficult to find a giant crater left by an asteroid that hit Earth 65 million years ago. The crater's traces might have been scraped away by erosion or covered up by land building. Or, the asteroid might have struck one of Earth's oceans. Oceans cover three quarters of

Earth's surface. Whatever remained of the impact could lie hidden beneath thousands of feet of water. Because of these problems, scientists have estimated that 90 percent of all large impact craters (greater than 6 miles or 10 kilometers in diameter) formed in the past 100 million years have yet to be found. Nevertheless, scientists set about the task of finding the smoking-gun *K-T crater*.

Although finding the crater would not be easy, scientists had an idea of what to look for. For centuries, astronomers had studied the moon and carefully mapped its craters. The crater Copernicus on the moon was an excellent place for comparison. Although smaller than the proposed K-T crater, the ancient Copernicus crater probably looks today like the missing Earth crater might have looked soon after it formed. The reason for the Copernicus crater's fresh look is that the moon has a very slow erosion rate. Features on its surface look pretty much the same today as they did hundreds of millions of years ago.

Copernicus is a large impact crater on the moon's near side. While not the largest crater on the moon, Copernicus is one of the best formed and easiest to see because it lies smack in the middle of the dark and smooth plains of the *Mare Imbrium*. Sunlight falling on the crater makes it stand out like a searchlight on a dark night.

The brightly lit walls circle a crater that is nearly 60 miles (almost 100 kilometers) across. The edge of the crater rim is sharp and has steep cliffs that fall in toward the crater's center. Inward from the rim are shelflike rock terraces, 1 to 5 miles (1.6 to 8 kilometers) wide, that slump downward. The crater floor is covered with hills, valleys, ridges, and winding cracks. In the center are several small mountains, uplifted when the moon's surface rebounded after the asteroid struck and blasted out the crater. Debris from the impact spread out around the moon, and large raylike piles of light-colored debris streak out from the crater's rim across the dark plain.

The moon's Copernicus crater, at the center of
this picture, can be seen clearly from Earth.

If it was like the Copernicus crater, the K-T crater would probably be a circular depression in Earth's surface. In its center would be a mound of broken and melted rock that had rebounded upward after the impact. It would have one or more rims, or *rings*, giving the crater a targetlike appearance. Near the hole's outer ring would be many parallel cracks where shelves of broken rock slumped down.

Debris from the blast would have fallen back in the crater's floor and piled up thickly for hundreds of miles around. If the asteroid struck an ocean, then the crater would exist on the ocean floor. However, there would be an additional feature. Huge ocean waves would have been driven outward from the impact. The waves would have crossed hundreds or thousands of miles to the continents, where they would have crashed on the shores with great force, flooded lowlands for perhaps hundreds of miles inland, and scrambled the land surface.

A WORLDWIDE SEARCH ▪ Large impact craters (but smaller than the ones the Alvarezes proposed) had been found on Earth's surface. Traces of a giant impact in Ontario's Sudbury Basin are still visible 2 billion years after the impact! The center of the 85-mile-wide (137-kilometer-wide) crater formed by this impact is now one of the richest mining districts in the world. The impact melted ancient rock, and this created the largest known deposits of nickel and huge deposits of copper and other valuable minerals. Also in Canada is the Manicouagan impact crater, some 60 miles (about 100 kilometers) wide, which formed about 210 million years ago. This crater is easily seen from airplanes and orbiting spacecraft. It is filled with water, forming a large ring-shaped lake.

Scientists were able to quickly eliminate both the Sudbury and Manicouagan impacts from their search for the K-T crater. Both impacts were much too old. The crater they were looking for had to be between 64 and 68 million years old. (The reason for the age spread is that methods of geologic dating are not precise. The 4-million-year spread would account for possible errors in dating.) In addition, the K-T crater had to be at least 100 miles (160 kilometers) across.

In this print from the 1800s, people marvel at
a meteor shower. Meteors are common, but most burn
up before impact—making craters rare on Earth.

In 1986, one geologist thought he had discovered the K-T crater. The Amirante Basin lying beneath the Indian Ocean is 180 miles (290 kilometers) wide and could have been formed by an asteroid impact. According to the geologist's reasoning, the impact may have triggered large lava flows that flooded the vast Deccan plateau in India about 65 million years ago.

After studying the thickness of deposits of debris believed to have been created by the K-T impact, other geologists felt the impact must have taken place on the other side of the world, somewhere in North America. This led scientists to farmland near Manson, Iowa.

In the 1950s, some strange rocks were discovered in the Manson area. Drill cores (rock cylinders cut out of deep holes by drilling equipment) showed rocks with mineral grains that were broken and cracked. At first, the discovery was misinterpreted. Geologists thought the cracks had formed when some deep underground volcanic explosion took place. In the 1960s, the rocks from the Manson cores were examined again. By then, geologists had a better understanding of how rock changes during an impact. The tremendous shock of an asteroid impact causes mineral grains to crack. When they looked again at the Manson cores, geologists realized that the farmland, consisting of 100 feet (30 meters) of soil brought down from the north by glaciers, covers a 21-mile-wide (34-kilometer-wide) impact crater.

At the time of the reexamination of the cores, no connection had been proposed between impacts and extinctions. But in the midst of the search for the K-T crater, some geologists remembered the Manson, Iowa, impact. Manson became a prime suspect for the smoking gun, but it didn't take long for geologists to reject it. Its location was right, but the crater was much too small to have been the site of the impact that caused the worldwide disaster leading to the dinosaur extinctions. At first, some scientists thought that the Manson impact could have taken place about the same time as the K-T impact, and the two might have combined forces to wreak greater havoc than either impact separately. However, the Manson crater was later found to be 75 million years old—too old by 10 million years.

In 1988, attention shifted to the Caribbean region. Scientists began looking there because of the discovery of coarse piles of rocky debris along the U.S. Gulf Coast, especially along the Brazos River in Texas. The scientists concluded that the debris was piled there by a huge ocean wave that could have been triggered by the crash of a great asteroid. By mapping the deposits, the scientists concluded that the impact might have taken place in the center of a 1,000-mile-wide (1,600-kilometer-wide) depression in the deep Caribbean Sea.

Important information was added when an 18-inch (45-centimeter) layer of pea-size claylike spheres was discovered in Haiti. Study of the spheres indicated that they were once rounded glassy pebbles called *tektites*. Tektites are often found near impact craters. The heat generated during the impact melts rock, and small globs of molten lava are sprayed into the air. The globs cool while falling to form glass pebbles in the shapes of spheres, tear drops, and even dumbbells. The Haiti deposit was very old and by the time it was discovered, the tektites had weathered into clay spheres.

Scientists were closing in on the smoking gun, but they still hadn't located it. Another proposed site for the impact was Cuba's Isle of Pines. The small circular island could have been created as the *central uplift* of a much larger crater that was now buried beneath the ocean. The scientists who proposed this idea had a problem confirming it. A check of the rocks of the island would show if there were any shock effects associated with an impact. But travel to the island was

Drill cores like these help scientists learn about Earth's history.

Tektites, formed by globs of molten rock, are common near impact craters.

restricted because it was once a maximum security prison. The site was later eliminated from consideration when rock samples from the island were located in a geological laboratory in Cuba. The rock showed no signs of intense shocks.

THE "TAIL OF THE DEVIL" ▪ Where to look next? Actually, the smoking gun crater had been discovered, but none of the geologists looking for it knew it. It had been found two years before the Alvarezes had published their hypothesis. In the spring of 1978, Pemex, the national oil company of Mexico, began a series of aerial magnetic surveys. With a *magnetometer* (a sensitive device that measures the strength and direction of magnetic fields) in tow behind a small plane, a mapping team crisscrossed the Gulf of Mexico north of the Yucatán Peninsula. Magnetometers provide geologists with a fast way of mapping the thickness of sedimentary rock over large areas. Such maps can help geologists locate oil deposits.

At the end of each day, Glen Penfield, a recently graduated geologist, examined the 15-foot (4.5-meter) strip charts that represented each 600-mile (almost 1,000-kilometer) pass of the magnetometer. After several successive days, Penfield began noticing a pattern in the magnetism. At first, the pattern was a small disturbance in the magnetic recordings. The next chart, taken a few miles to the south, showed a similar disturbance, but it was wider. In the third chart, the disturbance divided in two. On each successive chart the two disturbances were farther away, until they were almost 75 miles (about 120 kilometers) apart. At that point, a new disturbance appeared in the center of the charts. The pattern continued as the surveys crossed over the Yucatán Peninsula, with the disturbances first growing farther apart and then drawing together again to form the bottom of what was unmistakably a ring pattern. Penfield then

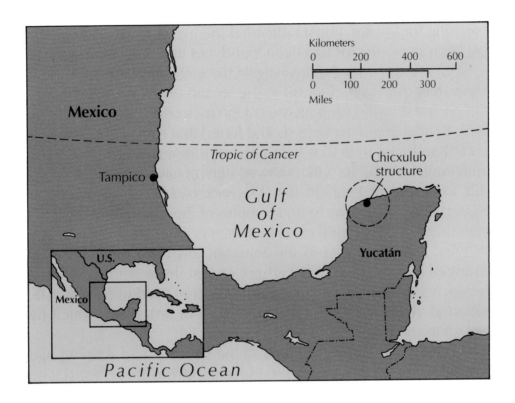

located gravity studies made of the area years earlier. They showed a ring structure that matched the magnetic ring measurements exactly! Penfield decided that what he was looking at was the structure of an ancient impact crater buried beneath thick layers of limestone. The northern half of the crater lay beneath the shallow waters of the Gulf of Mexico, and the other half underneath the northwestern side of the Yucatán Peninsula.

Penfield reported his discovery to the 1981 meeting of the Society of Exploration Geophysics. Although the report was well received there, nothing much happened because none of the scientists searching for the K-T impact attended the meeting. The crater they had been searching for had been found, but they didn't know it.

Penfield continued to investigate the crater. He discovered that Pemex had tried to drill for oil in the area in the 1950s. They didn't find oil, but they did keep records of the rock cores pulled up by the drills. Penfield read the records and found that the drill cut through more than half a mile (0.8 kilometer) of limestone rock before encountering a kind of rock that showed signs of having been shattered. This suggested to Penfield that the rock had been broken in an impact. He was anxious to find samples of the broken rock, but the warehouse where the drill cores had been stored had been destroyed in a fire. So he traveled to the Mexican town of Chicxulub (pronounced CHEEK-shoe-loob), where one of these wells had been drilled, in hopes of finding debris left over from the drilling. There he collected 30 pounds (about 14 kilograms) of limestone, which he sent off to some friends for analysis.

Meanwhile Alan Hildebrand of the University of Arizona had learned of Penfield's discoveries. Hildebrand was the scientist who had discovered the tektite deposits in Haiti. With Penfield's help, Hildebrand obtained some samples of a glassy broken rock that had been removed from one of the drill cores and sent to a geologist in the United States before the warehouse fire. Some of the samples indicated that they might have received intense shocks. The results were inconclusive, but here was another clue.

The National Aeronautics and Space Administration (NASA) added the next piece to the puzzle. In the early 1970s, NASA had begun launching a series of *Landsat* satellites to take pictures of the Earth's land masses. In 1987, a NASA scientist, Charles Duller, examined Landsat pictures and discovered a curious ring of water-filled sinkholes on the Yucatán Peninsula. Duller was looking for sources

Deep pools called cenotes dot the Yucatán region,
evidence of cracks in the limestone surface rock.

of water for the ancient Mayan Indian cities that were once located in the region. The sinkholes, called *cenotes* (pronounced seh-NOH-tays), were one source. Cenotes are cracks in the limestone surface rock that over time widened to form circular and elongated holes 300 to 500 feet (90 to 150 meters) in diameter. The thing that caught Duller's attention was that the holes formed a large semicircle across the Yucatán Peninsula. Cenotes lie outside the semicircle but not inside. Working with other scientists, Duller compared the semicircle with the circular magnetic pattern Penfield had discovered. The two patterns matched perfectly. From his studies, Duller hypothesized that the limestone that covers the land outside the semicircle had settled and cracked. The cracks eventually widened and filled with water to become the cenotes.

When all the scientific clues were assembled, it became clear that the smoking-gun crater everyone had been looking for had been discovered. Sixty-five million years ago, a huge rock from space smashed into Earth at a spot 18 miles (29 kilometers) northeast of the present location of the town of Chicxulub. Because of its closeness to the town, the K-T impact crater was renamed the Chicxulub Impact. The name is especially appropriate because Chicxulub comes from the Mayan Indian word that means "tail of the devil"!

TARGET EARTH

Chicxulub seems like an unlikely place for one of the greatest impact-caused explosions in the history of the world. The land covering the crater is relatively flat and consists of thick beds of limestone covered with a thin layer of soil. From the Gulf of Mexico to the Atlantic Ocean, the average width of the Yucatán Peninsula is no more than 200 miles (320 kilometers). Except for the water-filled cenotes, the land is hot and desert-dry, covered with farms and scrubby jungle.

The Yucatán Peninsula is home to the Maya Indians, who have inhabited the area continuously since 1500 B.C. The cenotes, a 65-million-year-old legacy of the K-T impact, attracted the Mayans, who built their cities and ceremonial centers nearby. Today, the peninsula is a land where tourists come looking for sandy beaches on the quiet blue waters of the Gulf of Mexico.

If we could scrape away the plants and soil from the northern end of the Yucatán Peninsula, push back the waters of the Gulf of Mexico, and excavate the limestone that covers the crater to a depth of 3,600 feet (1,100 meters), what would the impact crater look like?

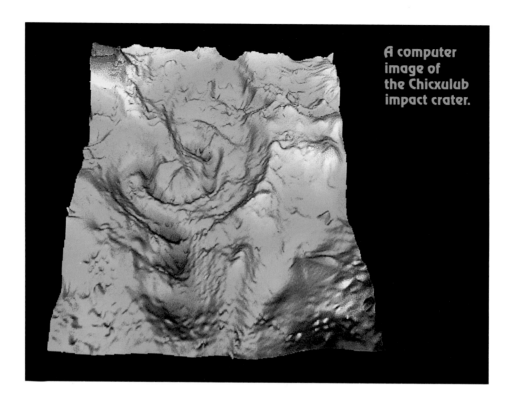

A computer image of the Chicxulub impact crater.

In a way, the crater has already been scraped clean. Scientists using *gravitometers*, devices that measure the local strength of Earth's gravity, have carefully measured the density of the rock beneath the surface. It is a way of mapping subsurface features.

A GIANT BULL'S-EYE ▪ The first thing you would see, with the limestone gone, would be an enormous circular basin 185 miles (298 kilometers) across. All of the islands of the state of Hawaii could easily squeeze within its ring, with the state of Rhode Island thrown in for good measure. However, if you were standing on the edge of the ring, you wouldn't know that it was a crater because you couldn't see to its other side. Because Earth is a huge sphere, the other side of the crater would lie beyond the horizon. The crater would just be too big to take in all at once.

The best place to see the whole crater would be from the vantage point of outer space. From a spacecraft orbiting hundreds of miles above the surface, the crater would look like a bull's-eye target. Instead of just one ring, you would see four rings. Inside that outer ring, or *rim crest*, that you were standing on is an *intermediate ring* approximately 130 miles (210 kilometers) across. Inside the intermediate ring is a *peak ring* approximately 92 miles (148 kilometers) across. Finally, in the very middle, is the fourth ring, or central mountain peak, about 65 miles (105 kilometers) wide. From the highest point on the outer ring to the lowest point on the crater floor there would be a total difference in elevation of about 11 miles (18 kilometers).

Back on the surface of the rim crest, you would notice just beneath your feet a thick layer of jumbled soil and shattered rock fragments. This is some of the rock debris that fell back down after it was kicked upward during the impact. As you look downward and in toward the crater's center, you would see wide shelves of rock that look like the edges of a row of toppled dominoes. Farther toward the middle of the crater would be more rock debris.

Since the crater's discovery, many scientists have studied it, and some have tried to estimate the force of the explosion that created it. One way to do that is to first determine the size of the object that struck Earth. By estimating how much iridium the asteroid deposited around the planet in the K-T clay layer, scientists have concluded the asteroid must have been between 5 and 6 miles (8 and 10 kilometers) in diameter—the same size the Alvarezes had proposed years earlier.

An artist's view of the moment of impact
as a huge asteroid collides with Earth.

The impact of the asteroid at Chicxulub must have been spectacular. It would have created an explosion with a force of well over 100 million *megatons* (equal to the explosion that would occur if 100 trillion tons of TNT were detonated all at once). Rock fragments, dust, and water vapor blasted out of the crater must have traveled upward into the atmosphere at speeds up to 25 miles (40 kilometers) per second. In seconds, thousands of cubic miles of pulverized rock dust reached up into the *stratosphere*, a layer of Earth's atmosphere that begins some 7 to 12 miles (11 to 19 kilometers) above the ground. In the process, trillions of tons of carbon dioxide and sulfur dioxide gases, contained within that rock, were released. Part of the energy of the impact was absorbed by Earth's crust, and powerful earthquake waves raced around the planet. Thousands of miles away from the impact, the waves snapped trees off at their base, triggered landslides and avalanches, and spilled water in lakes and rivers over their banks.

Because the impact took place along what is now the shoreline of the Gulf of Mexico, huge waves were driven across the Gulf. The waves contained so much energy that they washed up well into what is now central Texas before draining back into the Gulf. Shock waves of heated air, also generated by the explosion, spread outward, igniting into flames jungles and forests for thousands of miles around. The fires eventually burned off most of the vegetation on all the continents of Earth!

The dust in the atmosphere formed a dark cloud that blocked sunlight for many months to perhaps a year or more. Moisture in the air mixed with the carbon dioxide and sulfur dioxide gases. When rain fell, it was as corrosive as battery acid. Many plants and animals that had survived the initial impact, fires, and lack of sunlight died later because of the effects of acid rain.

NEW QUESTIONS ▪ Considering the discovery of the Chicxulub crater and the great catastrophe that accompanied its creation, one would think that the question of what caused extinction of the dinosaurs would finally be laid to rest. But that is not how science works. Scientists continue to question because there is always new evidence to uncover. Sometimes new evidence can completely change firmly established ideas.

For various reasons, some scientists have held on to the theory that dinosaurs were dying out on their own. By the end of the Cretaceous era, the dinosaurs were nearly done for, according to these scientists. At best, they feel, the K-T impact only pushed the dinosaurs over the brink of extinction. Other scientists think that all dinosaurs may not have died out but that some evolved into other life forms that exist today. Still others speculate that instead of one huge impact, several asteroids or several comets struck Earth over a period of a hundred thousand years. According to this hypothesis, each impact changed Earth's environment, making it difficult for many life forms to survive. Eventually, the changes accumulated to the point that most life forms could hold out no longer, and mass extinctions resulted.

One alternate theory takes us to the Deccan plateau in India. Starting as long ago as 68.5 million years, a series of massive volcanic eruptions is believed to have taken place there. The eruptions lasted for 3.5 million years, ending at the time of the K-T impact. During that time enough lava poured out of the ground to form a layer of rock 10 feet (3 meters) deep if it were spread evenly over Earth's surface. The new theory states that the eruptions would have played a major role in the dinosaurs' demise. Vast amounts of carbon dioxide and sulfur dioxide would have been released as the lava poured out from Earth's interior. Large amounts of carbon dioxide gas in the atmosphere would have trapped sunlight, causing the Earth to

Meteors rain down on the newly formed Earth in this painting. Impacts were probably common in the planet's early days, but evidence has been wiped out over time.

become much warmer than usual. Sulfur dioxide is poisonous, and it would have combined with moisture in the air to make acid rain. When the K-T impact took place in the Yucatán Peninsula, according to this theory, Earth's life-forms were already under great stress. The impact helped finish the job for many of them.

Research into the end of the dinosaurs will probably continue for many years. We may never know the whole story about the extinctions. The toughest question that proponents of new extinction theories will have to answer is not what killed 70 percent of the species of life on Earth, but how the other 30 percent survived.

In spite of the debates, there is one point that nearly every scientist agrees on: There was a K-T impact. It was not the first impact on Earth, nor was it the last. There must have been hundreds and perhaps thousands of large impacts on Earth since the planet formed out of the great cloud of gas and dust that became our solar system more than 4.5 billion years ago. Even though fewer than 150 craters have been discovered on Earth's surface, we can be sure the planet suffered thousands of impacts in its long history. A quick trip around the solar system can confirm that.

Starting with our nearest neighbor, the moon, we can easily see the huge circular *mares* (pronounced MAR-rays), large basins that were created by asteroid impacts four billion years ago. The rest of the moon is covered with thousands of craters of all sizes. A large asteroid struck the planet Mercury four billion years ago, and the impact formed the Caloris Basin. Today, it is a ring-shaped area 800 miles (about 1,300 kilometers) across, consisting of cracks and ridges. The rest of the planet has been peppered with smaller impacts. Venus has many craters, even though only the largest objects from space have survived passage through that planet's very dense atmosphere to impact on the surface. Smaller objects usually broke

Meteor Crater in Arizona was punched out by a chunk of iron hurtling from space.

apart miles above the surface, causing shock waves that jumbled the ground below. Mars has large craters, too, and so does nearly every moon in the solar system.

Of course, all these impacts could be millions or billions of years old. Do we know of any very recent impacts? Scientists have to study impacts close up to determine their age, and the only place they can do that is on Earth. Have there been any recent impacts on Earth? The answer is yes.

Approximately 50,000 years ago, a 10,000-ton iron meteor struck the Arizona desert to form the famous Meteor Crater. It left a hole more than three fourths of a mile (1.2 kilometers) across.

A small asteroid flattened forests and set off fires
when it exploded over Siberia in 1908.

Much more recently, in 1908, was the "Tunguska Event" in central Siberia. Scientists believe a small rocky asteroid, no larger than 200 feet (about 60 meters) in diameter, crashed through Earth's atmosphere and exploded about 5 miles (8 kilometers) above its surface. The explosion flattened about 500 square miles (almost 1,300 square kilometers) of forest and ignited intense fires. If such an object were to fall today over a place like New York City, millions of people might die, and it might cause hundreds of billions of dollars worth of damage to the city itself.

Realizing that asteroid, comet, and meteorite impacts have been relatively common over Earth's long history has led many people to a frightening thought. If impacts have occurred in the past, then why not in the future? Is Earth a target for one or more asteroids or comets orbiting the sun? What would happen to human life if another K-T-size asteroid smashed into Earth? Could we survive such an event?

SPACEGUARD SURVEY

When compared to the entire Earth, the Chicxulub impact crater seems insignificant. To appreciate its relative size, imagine having a world globe that is 16 inches (40 centimeters) in diameter. The crater would then be a small circle less than half an inch (1 centimeter) across—about the size of a small marble. And the asteroid that made that crater on the globe would have been smaller than a pinhead!

It's hard to accept that so much damage was done by the real asteroid, but its impact changed the future of the world. For humans, the impact had a positive effect. The impact, and whatever additional environmental factors may have been at work at the time, wiped out 70 percent of Earth's life forms. That made it possible for the mammals, the group of animals we are members of, to become one of the dominant classes of life on the Earth.

Other impacts may have had positive effects as well. Many scientists now believe that a huge impact more than 4 billion years ago may have broken off a large chunk of the Earth that eventually became the moon. Comets, close relatives of asteroids, may have brought to Earth some of the water that now fills our ocean basins.

An imaginary view of New York City's last moments, as the nucleus
of a comet 30 miles (48 kilometers) in diameter strikes Earth.

And meteorites may have brought some of the carbon-based chemicals that became the basis of life on Earth.

It appears we owe a lot to asteroids, comets, and meteorites. But what if another big asteroid or comet shows up? If it is large enough, and heading right for us, it could bring another mass extinction. Humans and many other living things would perish, and life on Earth would have to start over again.

It would seem like a good idea to learn as much as we can about Earth-crossing asteroids and comets, so that if any have Earth's name on them, we might have a chance to do something about them. Yet, as of this writing, the number of people around the world who are trying to locate potentially dangerous asteroids and comets is less than the number of people that staff a typical fast-food restaurant!

HUNTING NEOS ▪ The primary way to find out about asteroids and comets is to look for them with powerful telescopes. The main observatories where teams of astronomers are hunting these objects, called near-Earth objects or NEOs, are located in California, Arizona, France, Chile, Australia, and Ukraine. Each observatory team is engaged in a friendly rivalry to discover the most NEOs. During the 1970s, only a few NEOs were discovered each year, partly because so few people were looking for them. Today, several NEOs are discovered each month.

The hunting technique is relatively simple. During the two or three weeks surrounding the new moon every month, when the night sky is the darkest, astronomers take pairs of pictures of wide regions of the sky. The pairs are separated by a gap in time. When the films are developed, the pictures in each pair are compared with each other, using a special device that makes any object that moved stand out against the background of stars that do not appear to move.

NEO SIGHTINGS

Although current efforts to find NEOs are limited, there have been some spectacular and alarming successes. On May 21, 1993, Tom Gehrels of the University of Arizona Spacewatch team spotted the smallest and fastest asteroid ever to be seen through a telescope. Named 1993 KA2, the chunk of rock was almost 20 feet (6 meters) in diameter and whipped by Earth at 48,000 miles (77,000 kilometers) per hour, passing within 90,000 miles (145,000 kilometers) of Earth's surface! Had it entered Earth's atmosphere, it would have created a spectacular light show as it disintegrated. Had the asteroid been 15 or 20 times larger and hit the Earth, it would have created an explosive force a million times greater than the atomic bomb that destroyed Hiroshima at the end of World War II.

On August 10, 1972, an object 10 yards (9 meters) in diameter skipped through Earth's atmosphere and narrowly missed colliding with the surface. It left a burning streak through the air about 900 miles (almost 1,500 kilometers) long before it plunged back into space.

Asteroid 1989 FC, a rock half a mile (0.8 kilometer) in diameter, crossed Earth's orbit on March 23, 1989, shooting past the planet about twice the distance to the moon and missing Earth by just six hours. This was the second time in the twentieth century that an asteroid of that size had come so close. In 1937, the asteroid Hermes passed within 450,000 miles (724,200 kilometers) of Earth. A much larger asteroid named Toutatis, 3 miles (about 5 kilometers) in diameter, made a 2-million-mile (3.2-million-kilometer) approach on December 8, 1992.

An asteroid approaches Earth in this painting.

Measurement of the movement permits the object's orbit to be calculated. The unknown object is then compared to a table listing all known NEOs. If the object doesn't match the tables, it is given a name that identifies it by the year and half month when it was discovered and the order in which it was discovered. For example, the name "1994 CB" means that it is the second asteroid (B) discovered in the first half of the month of February (C) in the year 1994. (The first letter represents the half month. "A" means the first half of January and "B" is the second half of January. The letter "I" is not used because it looks too much like the numeral 1.) Later, the object might be given a special name like 1036 Ganymed or 1862 Apollo.

Another technique for hunting NEOs is to use light-sensitive electronic chips instead of film. These are similar to the chips or *charged-coupled devices* (*CCD*s) that are used in television camcorders. Light falling on the chips is converted to electric signals that are analyzed by a computer. The computer determines which objects are moving and calculates their orbits. This technique has enabled the University of Arizona's Spacewatch team to discover an average of two new NEOs a month. In spite of their success and that of two teams working with an 18-inch (46-centimeter) telescope on Mount Palomar in California, only about 200 large asteroid NEOs—greater than one-half mile (0.8 kilometer) in diameter—have been discovered. This is just a tenth of the number scientists believe exist. At the current rate of NEO discoveries, locating all will take centuries.

To speed up the discovery process, a panel of scientists prepared a special report for the National Aeronautics and Space Administration in 1992. In the report, they recommended that a long-term "Spaceguard Survey" be created to locate most of the large and many of the smaller NEOs over twenty-five years.

The team proposed that a network of six new telescopes, with mirrors 6 to 10 feet (2 to 3 meters) in diameter, be constructed. Furthermore, the panel proposed that the team of scientists operating the network be connected to an information system that would help them coordinate their observations and assist in calculating the orbits of the new discoveries. Two of the proposed telescopes would be built and operated by the United States and the rest by other nations around the world.

The report estimated that the cost of building the telescopes would be approximately $50 million. The cost to operate the telescopes would be another $10 million to $15 million per year. In other words, the total Spaceguard Survey would cost about $425 million over twenty-five years. That may sound like a lot. But because the proposed network would be an international effort, other nations involved would share the cost. The total cost of the survey would amount to less than ten cents for every person living on Earth today.

Over the twenty-five-year period, the panel expected the Spaceguard network to be able to identify at least 91 percent of all the large asteroids, 77 percent of all *long-period comets* (those with orbits lasting more than 200 years), and about 10 percent of the smaller asteroids that could threaten Earth. (The smaller asteroids are estimated to number 300,000.) If the calculated orbits of any of those objects put them on a collision course with Earth, knowing about the danger months or years in advance could save millions of lives.

INTERCEPTION ▪ Assuming that an NEO heading for the Earth is discovered, what do we do about it? A second panel of scientists tackled that question. The answer they arrived at had two parts. First, once the object was detected, additional information about it would be needed. The Spaceguard Survey could calculate its orbit and make some preliminary determinations about the object's size, but more precise information would be needed to divert its path.

One important bit of information would be the object's mass. If there were two barrels sitting on the floor, one filled with nails and the other with sawdust, which would be easier to move? An object made up of metal and rock would be much harder to stop or deflect than a similar-size object made up of rock and ice. Knowing the asteroid's mass would be important in deciding how to intercept it.

Another important bit of data would be the object's structure. Is it a solid mass, or does it have lots of fractures that could cause it to shatter into many smaller pieces, which would each head for Earth on its own? It would be much easier to deal with one object at a time than dozens.

To answer these preliminary questions, the second panel proposed the development of reconnaissance rockets that would carry scientific instruments out to the object. The instruments would study it and radio their findings back to Earth. After the nature of the object was understood, an interceptor mission would be sent out to meet the object and either destroy it or deflect it from its path. Deflection would shove the object into a new path that would carry it away from Earth.

There have been all sorts of strange and interesting ideas about just how to do that. One possible method would be to carry a bunch of rockets to the object and mount them on the object's surface, with the engine nozzles pointing upward. The rockets would be fired, shoving the asteroid into a new course. A similar idea is to build *mass drivers* on the object's surface. A mass driver is something like an electric roller coaster. It begins with a track that slopes upward to an abrupt end. Astronauts, or some sort of automated system, would load cars on the track with heavy rocks mined from the object's surface. Using the power of electromagnets, the cars would be accelerated up the track to the end. The car would stop at the end of the track, but its contents would be tossed into space. The action force of throwing the rocks upward would be balanced by an equal reaction force pushing on the object in the opposite direction. Of course, because the object would be much more massive than the rocks, it would move much less than the rocks. However, sending carload after carload of rocks into space would add up, and the object's path would be changed.

Still another interesting idea would be to attach to the object a thin sail several square miles in area. Held by cables, the sail would resemble a parachute and would catch the atomic particles that are thrown out into space by the sun. In time, the pressure of these particles on the sail would pull the object onto a new course.

The most practical idea discussed by the panel would be to use nuclear weapons to intercept the object. If the object were too large or too solid to destroy, one or more nuclear weapons could be exploded near the object. The intense pulse of energy released by the bombs would hit the near side of the object and vaporize its surface. As the vaporized material blew off the surface, it would propel the object in the other direction.

Of course, to make any of these techniques work, timing would be very important. It would take far less energy to alter an object's course when it was years away from collision with Earth than when it was only a few months away. Moving the object only a tiny fraction of a degree from its course years before an impact would result in the object passing several million miles away instead of hitting Earth. If the interception were to take place when the impact was only a few months away, perhaps 100 times as much energy would be needed to move the object to a safe new course. At any rate, the best time of all

Nuclear weapons might be used to change an asteroid's course. In this painting, explosions can be seen along the asteroid's lower edge.

to change the object's path would be when it was at *perihelion*, or at the closest point in its orbit to the sun. A change in the object's path at perihelion would have the maximum effect in changing the rest of its orbit.

Although the prospect of a large asteroid or comet striking Earth is frightening, not everyone is convinced we should spend the money needed to find NEOs and develop reconnaissance and interceptor spacecraft. Adding the cost of reconnaissance and interceptor rockets to the cost of the Spaceguard Survey raises the cost of the total effort by several hundred million dollars. Some experts believe this is just too much to spend when other scientific and social programs are short of cash. After all, what are the chances of a large asteroid or comet hitting Earth in the foreseeable future?

The panel of scientists that prepared the Spaceguard Survey decided to look at just that question: What is the probability that a person living today will be killed by an asteroid or comet impact? They came up with two answers. The first is the chance of someone being killed by a small impact similar to the Tunguska event in central Siberia in 1908. They calculated that the probability of this in any year is about one in 30 million. It must be remembered that cosmic impacts are very rare events, and hundreds of years could go by before the next object struck Earth. Nevertheless, if the object were to strike a large city, or ocean water near large coastal towns, millions of people could die at one time.

The probability of dying from a larger impact that would devastate the whole world is much greater. Even though large impacts take place only every half a million years or so, a quarter or more of the Earth's human population could die in such an event. The panel calculated that the probability of dying from a large impact in any one year is about one in two million—greater than the probability of dying in a jet airplane crash. Again, remember that these events are very rare. The probabilities are high only because of the great number of people who would die at one time.

It is difficult to know what to do. Should the Spaceguard Survey and the interception technology be developed, or should the money be spent on something of more immediate benefit? The Spaceguard Survey panel members would tell you that delaying the start of their work could be a terrible mistake. If the survey spotted just one NEO on its way to Earth in time to do something about it, their efforts would be justified. Waiting until the object was close enough for anyone to see in the night sky would be too late.

A GLIMPSE OF THE FUTURE

Television screens in newsrooms around the world flickered, and then the image of a white-haired woman, sitting at a long table, appeared. To her left was an American flag, and at her right was seated a gray-haired man. On the front of the table was a blue and red NASA insignia.

"Good morning. I'm Barbara Schwartz, public information chief at the Johnson Space Center. This morning's news briefing will outline *Project Intercept*. Before I introduce our speaker, I would like to review the events that have led up to NASA's decision to launch this mission.

"As you know, two years ago astronomers at the Hawaiian Spaceguard Observatory detected a previously unknown Earth-crossing asteroid. It was named 2027 DA. The asteroid has a diameter of 1.12 kilometers and is traveling at a speed of 27 kilometers per second with respect to the sun. Computer projections have determined that if the asteroid continues on its present course it will collide with our planet 690 days from today. When it reaches Earth, it will impact at a speed of nearly 50 kilometers per second. Although we can't be sure of specific details, it is expected that the resulting explosion will devastate Earth at ground zero. The asteroid will create a force equal to 10,000 megatons and blast out a crater at least 15 kilometers in diameter. If it strikes a metropolitan area like Baltimore/Washington, as many as 20 million people may die instantly. In addition, the ash and vapors created in the collision will blot out the sun for three to six months and drastically alter Earth's climate for years to come. A similar, though larger, impact 65 million years ago is believed to have led to the extinction of the dinosaurs. The impact of 2027 DA has the potential of destroying all of humanity."

"I would now like to introduce Dr. Thomas Jones. Dr. Jones is the world's foremost authority on asteroids and is a former space shuttle astronaut. He will briefly describe the mission to intercept the asteroid and then answer your questions."

The television camera panned to the left and focused in on Dr. Jones.

"Thank you, Barbara. For the past ten years, I have been managing a NASA program to send a manned spacecraft out to an Earth-crossing asteroid, or ECA as we call it. We want to conduct scientific study of the asteroid and evaluate possible space mining technology."

Charts and colored slides appeared on the television screen as Dr. Jones spoke.

"ECAs are storehouses for many needed mineral resources. If mining asteroids becomes economically feasible, there will be many benefits for humanity.

"The mission was nearly ready for launch when 2027 DA was discovered. The timing was fortunate because we have been able to redesign our trajectory so that we can rendezvous with 2027 DA when it is nearest to the sun in its orbit. Naturally, our first priority is to deflect the asteroid from its collision with Earth.

"*Project Intercept* is a six-person, long-distance spacecraft that will be launched from lunar orbit nineteen days from now. After a four-month voyage, the crew will rendezvous with 2027 DA as it travels through the inner solar system. By flying in formation with the asteroid, the crew will be able to conduct a scientific study of its nature and evaluate possible mining techniques that could be applied to other asteroids in the future.

"Following a brief study period of two weeks, the crew will take steps to deflect the asteroid's course. This will take place 534 days before the asteroid's projected collision with Earth. Five refurbished hydrogen bombs, left over from the last century, are being loaded on board the spacecraft. Based on the crew's scientific study, one or more bombs will be detonated on, in, or near the asteroid. The resulting energy pulse from the bomb or bombs will vaporize the nearest surface of the asteroid. The high-temperature gases that will be released by the asteroid as a result will provide a rocketlike thrust that will nudge 2027 DA slightly out of its current orbit.

"All we have to do is deflect the asteroid's course by one one-hundredth of a degree. This very small change will cause the 2027 DA to miss Earth by a distance of 175,000 kilometers.

"In spite of the importance of our undertaking, it is a relatively straightforward mission and we give it an 83-percent probability of success. I am now ready to take any questions you may have on the specific details."

The press conference continued for three hours as questions were received from reporters from nearly every country on Earth. Deep in space, asteroid 2027 DA continued its inward trek toward the sun. In the time it took to conclude the press conference, 2027 DA had closed the distance in its orbit to its collision point with Earth by more than 298,000 kilometers!

GLOSSARY

Asteroid—a rocky object, ranging in size from a few hundred yards to a few hundred miles in diameter, that orbits the sun but has no atmosphere.

cenotes—circular or crescent-shaped lakes in the Yucatán Peninsula.

central uplift—mountains that thrust up from the middle of a large impact crater.

charged-coupled device (CCD)—a solid-state light detector used in electronic camera systems.

comet—an object consisting of ice and rock that orbits the sun and gives off a gaseous atmosphere (tail) in the sun's heat.

crater—a depression in the surface of a planet or moon, created by the impact of an object.

Earth-crossing asteroid (ECA)—an asteroid that crosses Earth's orbit.

Earth-crossing comet (ECC)—a comet that crosses Earth's orbit.

erosion—the forces of wind, water, ice, chemicals, and biological activity that wear away rock and other surface materials of Earth.

gravitometer—a device for measuring the local strength of Earth's gravitational attraction.

intermediate ring—one of the inner rings of the Chicxulub crater.

K-T crater—the crater formed by the impact of a giant asteroid 65 million years ago, at the boundary of the Cretaceous and Tertiary periods.

Landsat—a series of satellites launched by the National Aeronautics and Space Administration to study the land surface of Earth.

long-period comet—a comet with a period, or orbit around the sun, of more than 200 years.

magnetometer—a device for measuring the strength of the magnetism in rocks.

mares—the broad lava-filled basins on the moon's near side.

mass driver—an electromagnetic device designed to hurl material into space.

megaton—an explosive force equal to one million tons of TNT.

meteor—a piece of space rock that enters Earth's atmosphere, making a streak of light as it burns up.

meteorite—a piece of a meteoroid that survives the passage through the Earth's atmosphere and lands on Earth.

meteoroid—a piece of space rock that resulted from the collision of asteroids or the breakup of a comet.

near-Earth objects (NEOs)—asteroids and comets that orbit in Earth's vicinity.

peak ring—the ring in the Chicxulub crater nearest the peak or central uplift.

perihelion—the point at which an object orbiting the sun is closest to the sun.

photosynthesis—the process by which green plants, in the presence of sunlight, convert carbon dioxide and water into oxygen and sugar.

rim crest—the outer ring of a crater.

rings—the circular rims surrounding an impact crater.

short-period comet—a comet with a period, or orbit around the sun, of less than 20 years.

stratosphere—a layer of Earth's atmosphere ranging between approximately 7 to 12 miles (11 to 19 kilometers) and 30 miles (48 kilometers) above the ground.

tektites—rounded, glassy pebbles that formed from molten rock kicked up by a large impact.

SUGGESTED READING

The following books will provide you with additional information about asteroids, comets, and meteoroids and about the extinction of the dinosaurs.

Brewer, D. *Comets, Asteroids and Meteorites.* New York: Marshall Cavendish, 1992.

Darling, D. *Comets, Meteors, and Asteroids: Rocks in Space.* Minneapolis: Dillion Press, 1984.

Dingus, L. *What Color Is That Dinosaur? Questions, Answers, and Mysteries.* Brookfield, CT: The Millbrook Press, 1994.

Fradin, D. *Astronomy.* Chicago: Childrens Press, 1987.

Kelch, J. *Small Worlds: Exploring the 60 Moons of Our Solar System.* New York: Julian Messner, 1990.

Norman, D. *Dinosaur!* New York: Prentice Hall, 1991.

Vogt, G. *Halley's Comet: What We've Learned.* New York: Franklin Watts, 1987.

INDEX

ABOUT THE AUTHOR

At NASA's Education Division at the
Johnson Space Center in Houston, Texas,
Gregory L. Vogt works with astronauts
in developing educational videos for
schools. He has written extensively
about astronomy and space exploration;
among his books for young readers are
two series from The Millbrook Press,
Missions in Space and Gateway Solar
System. A former science teacher and
executive director of the Discovery
World Museum of Science, Economics, and
Technology in Milwaukee, Wisconsin, he
holds bachelor's and master's degrees
in science from the University of
Wisconsin at Milwaukee and a doctorate
in curriculum and instruction from
Oklahoma State University.